D1196440

GRIT

poems by

Karen Luke Jackson

Finishing Line Press
Georgetown, Kentucky

GRIT

in memory of Janis Luke Roberts (1952-2016)
… a wonder unto many (Psalm 71:7)

ACKNOWLEDGMENTS

"Sacred Lineage," *Ekphrastic* 2018

Publisher: Leah Maines

Editor: Christen Kincaid

Cover Art: Della Farmer, facebook.com/dellavan

Author Photo: Erica Mueller, https://ericamueller.com

Cover Design: Elizabeth Maines McCleavy

Order online: www.finishinglinepress.com
also available on amazon.com

Author inquiries and mail orders:
Finishing Line Press
P. O. Box 1626
Georgetown, Kentucky 40324
U. S. A.

Table of Contents

Sacred Lineage

Pranksters were tasked with communal roles:
Heyokas striped black and white
disrupted fertility rites. African Pygmies
costumed in leopard skins amused Pharaohs.
A comic poked fun at the Emperor's plan
to paint the Great Wall of China.
Mutes, *Sannos*, and fools, *Stupidus*,
mined scandals for sketches
in ancient Rome. Jesters
charmed royal courts. Mimes,
jokers, harlequins, tricksters,
christened clowns in the sixteenth century,
curators of crazy wisdom.

Childhood Clues

~1~

The cowgirl outfit Santa left
was by far my favorite gift.
Pistols with pearl handles
and a holster hugged my hips.

I tried it on that Christmas day—
the shirt, the chaps, the boots.
A chin strap held my hat in place
as I searched for stolen loot

a bandit might have hidden
in camellias while I slept.
I wasn't afraid I'd be attacked
because I was Quick Draw Pete.

When Daddy aimed his camera
I posed in a riding stance,
reached for my guns, crossed my eyes,
and gave him one last chance

to save himself. He clicked the shutter,
dubbed me Dead Eye Dick,
warned I'd never shoot straight
if I kept pulling that trick.

~2~

Two friends shadowed me
when I biked to Cumbee Park
or shopped at the five-and-ten.

They told me their names—
Ting Kong and Vallock. No one
saw them but me. We had fun

planning puppet shows, creating
comedy skits. When Daddy built
a playhouse in the back yard,

we set up housekeeping and barred
my sister from entering. If I broke
a cup while drying the dishes

or talked too much at school,
I pinned the blame on them.
People refused to believe me.

Ting Kong and Vallock said
not to worry. I was okay.
God made me this way.

~3~

In second grade, the teacher
sat me in a corner,

flashed cards at me
repeatedly.

My brain rejected
letters lined up

left to right, reversed
those squiggles

…*was* became *saw*…

now looked like *won*

…or *one*…I couldn't tell

which…the words so blurred
my head hurt.

Kids called me
stupid, dumb

but laughed
at my jokes.

~4~

My long, blonde hair
and Mama agreeing
to help me learn the lines
landed me the role.

In a blue dress
and white apron, I fell
down Rabbit's hole,
joined Mad Hatter for tea.

~5~

Clara Bell from the *Howdy Doody Show*,
Freddie Freeloader on evening TV,
Lamb Chop & Hush Puppy
and a clown card, Clancey,
in an Old Maid deck
cheered me.

Debut

I wanted to be a mother
in *Cheaper by the Dozen*,
kids running
through a wild, happy home

or an actress starring
on Broadway,
in musicals.
Neither was to be.

Oh, I married my high school
sweetheart, Oscar, captain
of the football team,
and we had three fine sons.

Most days I busied myself changing diapers,
cheering at t-ball games,
even baked and sold homemade
cinnamon rolls,

but I was in misery trying to stifle
the antics of Dead Eye Dick,
resist the temptations
of imaginary friends.

One morning, at my dressing
table applying makeup,
I looked in the mirror, crisscrossed
my eyes, and saw a stranger.

"I'm Clancey,"
she announced.
"Let me out of here!"

I picked up lipstick, rosied
my cheeks, reddened my lips,
grabbed the eyebrow pencil and drew
circles at the corners of my mouth.

Weeks passed before I purchased
an orange wig; months before I talked
a friend into forming a gift and balloon
business—Roaring Good Ideas.

Customers paid extra for clown deliveries,
so Sandra, as Mopsy, and I, as Clancey,
strutted hospital corridors, gloved
hands juggling wrapped packages.

We slipped into classrooms ferrying
frosted cupcakes, blow-out whistles.
Would have performed without pay
just to see those faces.

Sandra was diagnosed with cancer.
During her fight, I stayed by her side.
She survived. Mopsy retired.
Clancey trudged on alone.

Sandra's Take

When cancer flared, doctors removed most
of my intestines. I lay flat on my back for days.

Oscar plastered a Tom Selleck poster on the ceiling
compliments of Clancey. Staring at that hunk, half-clad,

would heal me, Janis vowed, then said,
"Don't worry, we'll take the children."

As I recovered, husband at my side,
Janis and Oscar doubled their brood,

fed my kids, bathed them, drove them to school
(some days on time), prayed I'd live.

I hated to retire Mopsy.
Janis said she understood.

Don't get me wrong: I liked Clancey,
but it was the woman I loved.

When my strength returned, our families
worshipped together, celebrated Christmases,

piled into a van headed to FSU games. When the home
team fell behind, Janis would stand on a stadium bench,

lead fans in a Tomahawk Chop and the Seminole War Cry—
a skill perfected when Oscar wore garnet and gold—

or line out a cheer resurrected from our high school
days, on the sidelines, shaking pompoms, red and gray.

She typed church bulletins, carried meals to shut-ins,
hosted baby and bridal showers. Her home a haven

for teens who cannonballed into the backyard pool,
grabbed burgers off the grill. My children claimed

Janis was their second Mama;
Oscar her Prince Charming.

Grit

Steering down a two-lane country road in a jump suit
covered with polka dots—green, yellow, and pink—
a Halloween costume grabbed from a sales rack at Walmart,
did Janis's mind wander back to that lock-down ward, a week

on suicide watch? "Tired of dusting," she'd said when asked
why she'd ripped the doors from their brackets, raked the pantry
clean of refried beans, Lay's Potato Chips and Little Debbie cakes.
She refused shock therapy but swallowed pills to muffle the angry

voices vying in her head, came home and crawled into bed to grieve
the balloon bouquets and singing telegrams she'd lost.
Two years later, a newspaper article offered a glimmer of relief.
"Southeastern Clowns Converge in Bainbridge: *Puttin' on the Grits.*"

"I'm going," she said when Oscar asked how her day had been.
"We both know I won't get well until I laugh again."

Cronies

One loyal friend is worth ten thousand relatives.
Euripides

My friend, Mama Clown, born in Columbia,
South America, now living in Miami, paints children
into butterflies, princesses, and Ninja
Turtles. At *Puttin' on the Grits*, she fashioned
a new Clancey face. Everything else—
costume, shoes, funny routines—
she swore would manifest like magic.
She also taught me to curse in Spanish.

My "big brother" Buttons, Ringling's advance man
for seven years, touted *The Greatest Show on Earth*.
His weirdest gig: rope tricks for monks.
Tired of the road, he moved to West Virginia
with his wife and sons. There he earned his living
teaching First of Mays, bottling makeup
remover, and manufacturing bulbous noses.
Now he entertains as Old Saint Nick.

Pinky, closer than a sister and more fun too,
grew up in South Carolina too poor to buy
a pole, so she fished with string. Now she reads
to jailed mothers, duets with her puppet Cilly,
and smuggles medicine through customs
for Ukrainian orphans. Her homemade
biscuits topped with blackberry jam
fortify like communion bread.

Clown Shoes

You should've seen that gal
    when she tried us on
    at the dealer's table,
waving her arms like a windmill,
tripping over our laces, falling

forward. She soon steadied, strode with
    a lopping gait, our
    flopping toe boxes
a world of rainbows and crayoned hearts
that delighted children. With each goofy

step, her real heart cracked
    open, inch by inch,
    wearing her out, us too.
She was buried in her clown costume,
barefoot. We still live in her walk-in closet.

Smileville

Born in a different place or time, Janis might have designed
for Disney, penned fantastic stories like Sendak and Dahl,
so vivid was her imagination (or was it Clancey's mind?)
that conjured Smileville, in the State of O'Silly. No small

task to concoct a town where clouds rain ribbons and kids
take cotton candy carpet rides. Notions for an amusement park
or feature cartoon. A feed store selling donut seeds. Hobos fizz-
ing soda pop. Need a laugh? Drop by Nurse Goodbody's Clinic;

have Ferm Perm streak your hair. Bored? Tour the pink
courthouse where the mayor welcomes guests. Take a field
trip to dig for gummy worms. Feeling out-of-sync?
Visit the Chapel of Cheer, leave singing. A world so real

children begged for directions, and she obliged.
Turn right at a lollipop light. Glide down a taffy slide.

A Minute for Children

1. Homeless, Tent City, Miami, Florida

After the hurricane, we lived
in tents, sidestepped
trash to line up
for food, a cup

of soup, some bread. I hated nights
most—no street lights,
sirens' shrill roars.
Imagine four

clowns coming to entertain us,
pockets in suits
filled with sweet treats.
Best gift—glow sticks.

2. Patient, Scottish Rite Hospital, Atlanta, Georgia

When Clancey visited our ward,
no one was bored.
Balloons in hand,
bright-eyed, she scanned

the beds, came to rest on my head,
bald, tray of meds
on nearby cart.
"I'll bet you're smart,"

she said, then made coins disappear,
pulled scarves from ears.
Better than pills.
Forgot I was ill.

3. Preteen, White House Easter Egg Roll, Washington, D.C.

Clancey invited me to go.
I'm her niece, so
I begged my dad
'til he agreed

but only if I carried mace.
Kept a straight face
when frisked by guards.
Took more than words

to dodge arrest. Peanuts, Georgia
grown, wrapped in foil,
set off alarms—
a clown's ransom.

Reality Check
after an elementary school performance

I was home washing clothes
when the phone rang.
"Miss Janis," the child said,
"Is Clancey around?"

I'd told the kids that Janis
was Clancey's manager
(although sometimes
it seemed the other way around),
didn't want to disappoint,
lowered the receiver,
switched to my stage voice.

"Hello, young man,"
Clancey boomed.
"Glad you caught me
before I left town."

I waited to be asked
about coming to his birthday party
or for a balloon twisted into
a Luke Skywalker lightsaber
the next time I visited his class.

Instead, he said, "Clancey, can I go
with you and live in Smileville?"

I cranked up my usual patter, how
Smileville was a place in his heart
he could visit when he was sad
or afraid.

"But *you're real*, Clancey!"

His plea chilled my spine, sent Clancey
reeling. Then the child shared—
no food in the house, hiding
in closets, belt buckle beatings.

Clancey promised to help,
hung up,
wept.

I called the school counselor,
watched
as he was placed in foster care.

For years, Clancey searched for this boy
at school events, visited with stuffed
animals when he was sick. He never
asked to live in Smileville again,
but he ate dirt cake from the town's
Bake Shoppe and learned
how to plant donut seeds,

and like the Velveteen Rabbit,
the Clown learned
a child made her real.

A Sister's Rx

When my marriage failed,
Janis declared clowns
good medicine, convinced
me to join her at a Christian
clowning conference.

I showed up in a red power suit
with patent pumps—a disguise,
her clown friends alleged, for
    a whiteface or
    a hobo living inside.

In a magic class, I sneaked
behind my sister's chair, yanked
a giant baseball cap
gussied with yellow brim
from Janis's rumpled hair,
    bolted toward
    the dealers' tables.

She could've chased; instead,
forgave the theft, watched
Mama Clown dab white
greasepaint round
my mouth and eyes,
pencil arches for brows.

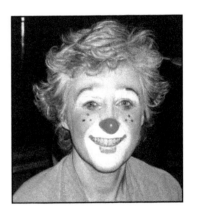

The moment my nose
was glued in place—
    Shazam! Spunky!
        a newborn clown—

a freckle-faced tomboy
in cut-off overalls and striped
socks stretched thigh-high,

a tree hugger who traded trinkets,
pocketed a slingshot, Goliath-size,
and fended off pie ambushes
with a water-squirting frog.

*More fun than being
an adult,* I jived.

Spunky steered clear of skits,
never sculpted a balloon
into a poodle, preferred to
upstage Clancey when she
was on mayoral business.

Wingman

When Janis launches a show
I hug the back of a room,
scan laughing faces,
and shake my head
at the lines
that pop
from my wife's mouth.

Today it's Nurse Goodbody's turn,
Clancey's second-in-command,
to roast a dentist in a nearby town.

As I drive the van, loaded with props
gleaned from the house,
Janis rummages through a medical bag,
gift from a large animal vet,
extracts a six-inch hypodermic
"to deaden his jaw," she says,

then asks, "what should I use
to pad his gums?"

The staff, all women,
have disclosed their boss's pet peeves
and curious habits, fodder for an act
now scrolling in her head.

We sneak inside.
I shoulder a camera, capture the dentist's
headlight-stare as Nurse Goodbody grabs
his elbow, guides him to an exam room
and seats him in the chair.
Bookkeepers and hygienists
crowd the space. Even his wife
is there.

A tinge of sympathy flickers
for this man. I've seen Janis at work;
it's easier for those who play along,
but he's pissed. As she sheaths him

with a shower curtain, he sneers,
makes a suggestive remark. I fumble
filming, recover as
Goodbody lifts a garden hose,
pretends to flush his mouth.

The dentist sputters, tries to rise,
end the show,
but she pins him with one hand,
and with the other
reaches—not for the bag
of fluffy marshmallows—
but for the box
of feminine hygiene
products
with daisies on the front.

Bespangled

When cummings wrote about a bespangled clown
at the magical hour when is becomes if,
he described my sister's ethereal soul,
a mystery for which i've no words.

Characters sprang from her head
completely alert and miraculously whole,
like Athena from Zeus, fully grown, fully armed
and *anything but dumb.* Like Athena,

Janis was a father's daughter:
outgoing and protective and wise,
her hug an engulfing love.
No one escaped when wheels spun

in her head. Thank heaven she acted crazy.
Thank heaven she passed out daisies.

Coulrophobia

A term concocted
in the 1980s
to describe terror
of painted faces;

from the Greek *kolon*,
or limb, an unlikely stretch
from flailing legs
to petrifying stilt walkers;

ignoring *skero-paiktes,*
the ancient Greek word
for clown
or to play like a child;

popularized by
ihateclowns
websites that advocate
clown-free zones.

Diabolical Descent

Dickens bears some of the blame.
Editing the memoirs of Joseph Grimaldi,
London's first modern clown, he harvested
tragedies of father and son, planted
suspicion that whiteface gaiety
masks misery, pain.

Or consider Deburau, a renowned French mime,
who employed a cane instead of a limb
to beat a boy to death for taunting him.
Acquitted of murder at the time.
Or *Pagliacci*, a cuckolded clown who stabbed
his unfaithful wife, on stage.

And in Clancey's time, there's John Wayne Gacy,
Pogo his registered name. Easy access to children.
Executed for 33 crimes.
Tricksters, dark and malicious, now haunt
screens: *Batman's* Joker. *The Simpsons'* Krusty.
Pennywise in Stephen King's *It*.

In Defense of Clowning

Clowns with a sad streak, I understand.
Take Joe Grimaldi. He lampooned high fashion
on Sadler's stage. His telling line, "I'm Grim
all day, so you can laugh all night."

Or Emmet Kelly's Weary Willie
whose five o'clock shadow,
Depression-born,
echoed the nation's pain

and Robin Williams, a clown who portrayed
another, Patch Adams. Both spread laughter
to aid healing. Like Proverbs says,
a merry heart is good medicine.

I teach students to scan a crowd,
give adults who hang back a wide berth.
With skittish tykes, I pretend
to be scared of humans, lower my voice.

If they're still shy, I kneel or crouch
and ask, *are you married?*
The question yields a quizzical look
or a chuckle. Puts them in charge.

It almost killed me when my grandchildren
recoiled from Clancey. I tried what Ringling
clowns did: let them watch me pat my face
with flesh-toned make up, dab on white cheeks,

pencil a red mouth and add black exclamation
points over both eyes. Even had them swab glue
on the inside of the nose, then press the bulb
on mine. After that, whenever Clancey appeared,

they clapped and cheered. I'm glad they did
because, Lord knows,
I needed a clown's heart
to hold this world's despair and ecstasy.

Laying Down the Law

Don't know how Janis summoned
the courage to board that Atlanta plane.
I was sure she'd drive.
Would've gone if asked
but her sister's not afraid to fly.

Years ago, her daddy and I
cruised with the clowns to the Bahamas.
Mama Clown painted him a hobo,
me a whiteface.
Pegged us both right.

And we piggybacked a trip
to Branson where Oscar
chauffeured us to shows
while Janis taught classes.
Imagine that!

One night, at dinner with her friends,
a rigged table rose slow
as a snail crawling up a gutter.
I didn't notice 'til the soup bowl
hit my chin.

I preened like a bantam hen
when those Texas clowns
asked Janis to keynote their state
convention, in Midlands no less,
home to oil men and President Bush.

After my daughters returned,
I declared I'd die if they ever flew
in the same plane again,
never mind they were middle-aged
and I in my seventies.

Flying High

The flight from Atlanta
smooth
or could've been the Xanax
Janis swallowed.
Whitley pills
we called the white tablets
named for the jittery side
of our family.

But she hadn't downed
enough downers to face
the puddle jumper
awaiting us in Dallas.

I offered to rent a car,
drive the rest of the way
even though
it would've made us late.

She refused,
walked the tarmac
as if it were a plank,
then froze.

Calling on her inner clown,
she straightened her spine,
cracked her knuckles,
and, with eyes
a little too bright,
climbed the metal steps,
and gave a Presidential wave
before ducking through the rabbit hole.

I trailed behind.

In the cabin
she spied a pilot
sitting in the back,
deadheading a ride.

"Don't you have to be up front
to fly this bird?" she quipped.

Fueled by the laughter
of fellow passengers
she launched her Smileville patter.

I led her to her seat,
tried to shush
her flow of words,

but after take-off
she unbuckled her belt
and roamed the tight space
spinning stories
like the propellers outside
the entire forty-minute ride.

A Fan's Tip of the Hat

to Janis Luke Roberts
who shouted *Hey Everybody*, her
signature greeting whether festooned
as a clown or dressed in t-shirt and jeans
as she swept into a local diner or onto a stage.
Fans watched her bloom into a performer like Red
Skelton, a 1950s quick-change artist who'd turn his
back, don teeth, glasses or hat then reappear a different
thespian. She mimicked his trick in her Clown Nutty
News Network skit, playing all parts: black bifocals for
the evening anchor, a red Falcon's cap atop the noggin
of a loud-mouth sportscaster, in the soap commercial
tying an apron round her waist and brandishing a mop,
then closing as an umbrellaed weather girl chasing
cloud patterns, raining laughter down. At her zenith,
winning accolades from North American colleagues and joeys from Down Under,
de-stressing parents, teachers, and doctors with full-hearted merriment,
trumpeting *I love every bone in your body…especially your funny bone.*

Headlines

When I heard Miss Janis had died, I knew
I'd write the story. I attended high school with her boys,
played baseball with Luke, her middle son. We wore
Clancey the Clown Loves Me t-shirts
under our uniforms. Brought us luck.

On game days, Clancey'd storm the cafeteria
hunting students who crouched under tables.
In her striped pants, blue coat, and top hat sporting
a white mum, she towered six feet. As classmates
ratted, Clancey would kneel, grab an ear

like a first-grade teacher, haul out a game-winning
athlete, and plant a kiss on his cheek. She promised
to love us to the rainbow and back, no matter
how old we got or how big. Then she'd sing
the school fight song and lead a cheer.

After graduation, I signed on as cub reporter
for *The Ocilla Star.* My favorite assignment—
covering Clancey at birthday parties, library shows,
the Sweet Potato Festival, and her most famous gig,
the White House Easter Egg Roll. She quipped

she was going to "hunt for Quayle in the Bushes."
On the lawn, weatherman Willard Scott and Clancey posed
nose to nose. That photo claimed the local rag's front page.
I wonder how Mr. Oscar's faring. The whole town's in shock.
Miss Janis was the closest thing we've ever had to a rock star.

Take Two

If that late-night call
        had been a scene in a movie,

I'd have asked the director
        for a reshoot

from the moment I let my sister dangle
        on the phone, so weary

was I of listening. She tried to tell me
        she was tired of living,

checking off last things to do.
        I refused such news,

insisted she was fine—
        the lymphoma in remission,

had to be depression talking—
        and began naming her blessings

one by one
        like the old hymn taught:

good husband, roof over her head,
        food on the table,

and all the while my lips puckered
        like they did when as kids

we sucked sour juice from green grapes
        that grew along Aunt Ruth's fence,

and my voice grew as sharp
        as a butcher knife.

Great Timing

~1~

For two years after Daddy died
I hunkered in bed most days
battling lymphoma,
whooping cough, shingles
in my ears and eyes,
degenerative discs from poorly
executed pratfalls.

But I managed to visit
the Blue Ridge Mountains,
attend an international clown
convention, and swim with dolphins,
all bucket-list items.

After Oscar converted the one-room
school house Mama had attended as a child
into a playhouse for our grandkids,
I knew my time had come.

~2~

I rode a kidney infection
to my death. After surgery to remove
stones, sepsis set in. The doctors hooked
me to a vent but poison flooded
my bloodstream. Major organs
failed. So quick my demise,
I had no time to say goodbye.

Guess that's why God
let me hang around.

Before the funeral, I floated above
the crowd. The sanctuary hummed
but folks quieted their chatter
when Oscar edged
to the open casket.

A floral spray
with a balloon bouquet
rested near the coffin—
too tempting.

When a balloon popped,
a cousin chimed
"She's here!"
Even Oscar smiled.

Down the Road

Janis banned goodbye, a vulgar word in her lexicon,
insisted kin, strangers, and friends say *Down the road,
bump a nose* as they parted. No danger you'd hear common
farewells like *see you later* or *so long* when she dismissed

a class or rose from the table after a meal, so headstrong
her conviction that life transcends death, the show must go on,
a circus send-off not unlike her father's songs
and Eskimo kisses as he left for work, his return foregone.

When Janis entered the heaven she'd envisioned,
her Chapel of Cheer became a Temple of Joy.
There she paints rainbows that beam like the prismed
pants that Clancey wore and star streaks indigo

skies, trills with archangels and scatters charms,
hovers as lovers fall into each other's arms.

Obituary

excerpt from The Ocilla Star, *June 1, 2016*
written by Sandra Sumner ("Sandra's Take")

Janis Luke Roberts was born on August 31, 1952, in Ocilla, Georgia to O. L. Luke, Jr. and Eloise Royal Luke of Irwin County. She went to be with the Lord on May 25, 2016, in Tifton, Georgia. In mid-1981, Janis had a vision that would change her life and the lives of those around her. She became Clancey the Clown, delivering balloon bouquets and singing telegrams to people of all ages. Janis, a devoted wife, loving mother, cherished Anma, and faithful friend, leaves behind her loving husband of almost 45 years, Oscar Roberts. The homegoing service celebrating her amazing life was held at her beloved Frank Primitive Baptist Church in the presence of an overflowing crowd of family and loved ones, including her closest clown friends.

Special Thanks

"Clown Shoes" appeared five months after my sister's death in a class that Ken Chamlee taught in the UNCA Great Smokies Writing Program. I hadn't planned to write about Janis or Clancey, but fellow students begged for more. So, for the next two years, as I grieved her loss, I penned poems about her life as a clown.

I am grateful to Ken, Cathy Smith Bowers, Tina Barr, Pat Riviere-Seel, and Eric Nelson, who have taught me much about writing poetry and who workshopped many of these poems. Also, gratitude goes to those who read first drafts of poems and subsequent revisions, especially Anne Westbrook Green, Emily Wilmer, Jane Curran, Kathy Nelson, Rebecca Ethridge, Kathleen Calby, Nancy Holmes, Nancy Pemberton, Catherine Gillett, and Greg Lobas.

This collection would not have come to fruition without the ongoing encouragement of Tonya Staufer, who met my sister in college and came to know every clown character Janis portrayed. Thank you, Tonya, for sharing memories with me as words flowed onto the page.

To my sister's angel, Theresa Garrett (Pinky the Clown), I owe a debt of gratitude for the times you brought joy and healing into my sister's life and to Marcella Murad (Mama Clown) and Leon McBryde (Buttons) who taught Clancey the fine art of clowning.

With her husband, Oscar, by her side, Janis's gifts flourished. Thank you, brother-in-love, for supporting my sister and living in her make-believe world. And to the people of Ocilla, who adored and championed Clancey, especially Sandra Sumner, may these stories and the laugher Clancey spread live on.

Cover Art Note

Della Farmer, Ocilla, Georgia, a cousin who considered Janis her aunt, painted the cover portrait the night following my sister's death. Clancey had appeared at many of her birthday parties. She chose to paint the clown, rather than the woman, to remember the light and laughter Clancey had spread. "The eyes," Della's mother Dale observed, "were Janis's whether she was in street clothes or costume." When the portrait appeared with the front-page article about Janis's passing, hundreds of people in Irwin County asked for copies. Della made them available at no cost. "Sharing Clancey's love," the artist said, "that's what Aunt Janis taught me." The original painting graces my study. There Clancey watched and prodded as these poems emerged. Thanks, Della!

Karen Luke Jackson's oral history background, educational experience, and clowning escapades provide a latticework for her life's work. Whether crafting a poem, raising money for a nonprofit, or leading contemplative retreats, Karen searches for life-giving "role/soul" connections. Writing, she believes, allow us to explore the core of our human experience and capture snippets of sacred mystery in everyday life.

An award-winning poet, Karen's work has appeared in numerous journals including *Broad River Review* (Ron Rash Poetry Award), *Ruminate* (Janet McCabe Poetry Award, Honorable Mention), *Kestrel, One, Emrys Journal, Friends Journal, Christian Feminism Today, Presence: An International Journal of Spiritual Direction, eno, TOWN Magazine, The Pisgah Review, moonShine review, The Great Smokies Review, Kakalak,* and several anthologies. She also co-edited *The Story Mandala: Finding Wholeness in a Divided World.* A native of Ocilla, Georgia, Karen is currently working on a memoir that spans six generations.

Karen holds a doctorate in education from North Carolina State University and is a facilitator with the Center for Courage & Renewal and the Center for Renewal and Wholeness in Higher Education. She recently downsized to a cottage on a goat pasture in Western North Carolina. When she's not writing or sitting in circles, she companions people on their spiritual journeys. Being a grandmother to Jackson, Kaia, and Auden and living in the Blue Ridge Mountains are two of her greatest joys.

For more information, visit Karen's website:
https://www.karenlukejackson.com